AF668226

My First Book of

Alphabet

Creative Head: Sanjay Dhiman **Concept by:** Deepika Jain
Designed by: Chandan Kumar **Image Researcher:** Neha Tiwari

Aa

Apple

Aeroplane

Arrow

Axe

Bb

Ball

Bucket

Butterfly

Banana

Cc

Car

Cup

Clock

Cat

Dd

Doll

Duck

Dice

Dog

Ee

Elephant

Ff

Fan

Fish

Gg

Goat

Grapes

Eagle

Eggs

Envelope

Fruit

Flower

Gloves

Girl

Hh

House

Hen

Hat

Horse

Ii

IGLOO

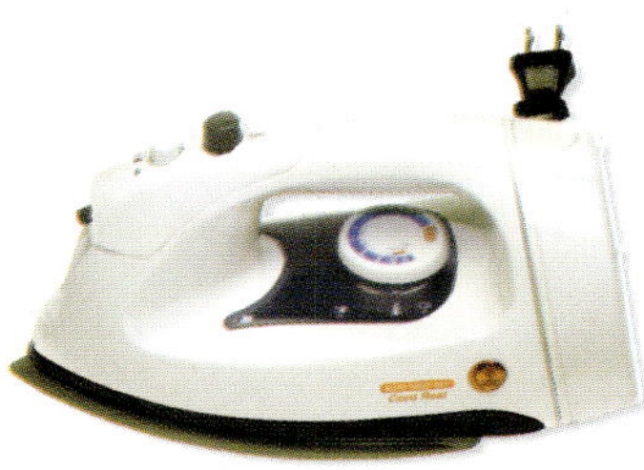

Inkpot

Iron

Ice cream

Jj

Joker

Juice

Jelly

Jug

Kk

Koala

Kid

Keys

Kettle

Ll

Lion

Lemon

Mm

Mask

Monkey

Nn

Nest

Nut

Lamp

Leaf

Mug

Mouse

Night

Nib

Oo

Orange

Owl

Oil

Onion

Pp

Panda

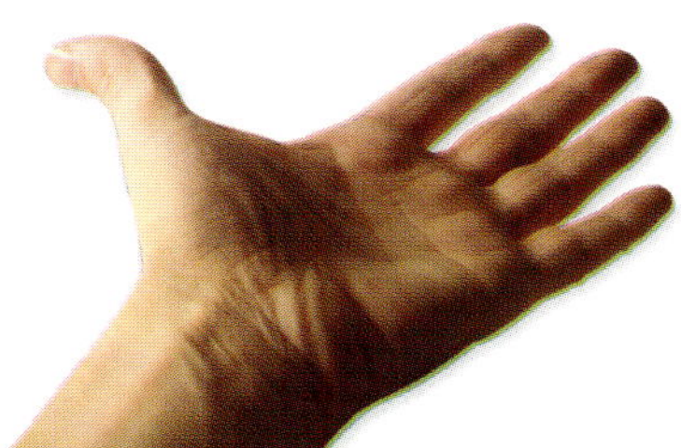

Palm

Pear

Parrot

Qq

Queen

Quail

Quilt

Quiet

Rr

Rainbow

Rabbit

Rose

Ribbon

Ss

Snowman

Strawberry

Tt

Telephone

Tiger

Uu

Umbrella

Uniform

Sun

Star

Tomato

Teddy Bear

Up

Utensils

Vv

Vegetables

Vase

Violin

Van

Ww

Whale

Worm

Watermelon

Watch

Xx

X-mas
Tree

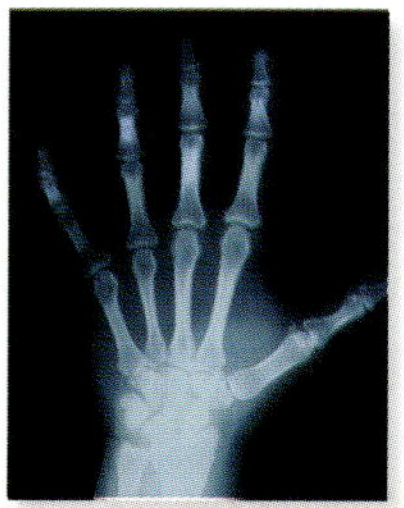

X-ray

Xylophone

Xerox

Yy

Yak

Yarn

Yo-yo

Yolk

Zz

Zebra

Zero

Zip

Zig-zag